GW00601060

Contents

Radiating Christ
978-0-9570793-3-5

Nihil Obstat: Father Anton Cowan, Censor
Imprimatur: The Most Reverend Vincent Nichols, Archbishop of Westminster
Date: Feast of St Matthew the Evangelist, 21 September 2012

The Nihil obstat *and* Imprimatur *are a declaration that a book or pamphlet is considered to be free from doctrinal or moral error. It is not implied that those who have granted the* Nihil obstat *and* Imprimatur *agree with the contents, opinions or statements expressed.*

Writing Group: Dr Mark Nash, Ms Clare Ward, Mrs Margaret Wickware
With thanks to Frs Michael O'Boy, Simon Penhalagan and Gerard Sheehan for comments and suggested edits and to Miss Carolyn Wickware and Mr Henry Tregidgo for the 'Exploring our Heritage' timeline on pages 52-53.

The Westminster Diocesan Agency for Evangelisation is grateful to the National Council of the Churches of Christ in the U.S.A for use of the New Revised Standard Version Bible: Catholic Edition copyright © 1993 and 1989. Excerpts from The Divine Office © 1974, hierarchies of Australia, England and Wales, Ireland. All rights reserved.

All of the images contained in this booklet have been taken from those freely available at the Wikimedia Commons website and from diocesan stock.

Produced by Agency for Evangelisation, Vaughan House, 46 Francis Street, London, SW1P 1QN. Tel: 020 7798 9152; email: evangelisation@rcdow.org.uk

 booklets are published by WRCDT. Design by Mark Nash.
Printing by The Graphic Design House Tel: 02392 334971

The Diocese of Westminster's Agency for Evangelisation is committed to a sustainable future for our planet. The booklet in your hands is made from paper certified by the Forest Stewardship Council.

Foreword

Dear brothers and sisters,

In this Year of Faith, which the Holy Father has announced and which represents a wonderful opportunity, I have asked each parish and school to consider taking on a project, according to their particular circumstances, to deepen our understanding of our faith. As important as these projects and larger events, is the personal challenge to determine where we might learn a little more about our Faith, examine how what we believe impacts on our behaviour and how we may witness to Jesus Christ in a world yearning for what he offers.

True discipleship requires thought, assent to the gift of God's grace and a response in love. We are offered no less than Jesus Christ, the Way, the Truth and the Life. It is he who has changed all of history through his incarnation, his passion, death, resurrection and ascension. It is he who can change us just as radically if we enter into and seek to deepen our relationship with him.

Blessed John Henry Newman understood this so very well and expressed it beautifully though poetry and prose. His *Radiating Christ* is a powerful invitation and reminder that each of us to pray for the grace to shine with the presence of God to all we meet. Such witness must be characterised by love, hope and joy, for we have not been gifted something dull and lifeless but vigorous and grace-filled.

Therefore, I ask families, in this Year of Faith, to come together to explore the themes of this booklet. I invite groups to open their doors to new members. I encourage each individual to take up the challenge of their baptismal calling and radiate Jesus Christ, our Lord and Saviour, to those we meet day by day.

Yours devotedly,

+ Vincent Nichols

The Most Reverend Vincent Nichols
Archbishop of Westminster

Radiating Christ

About this book

'By faith, the Apostles left everything to follow their Master (cf. Mark 10:28). They believed the words with which he proclaimed the Kingdom of God present and fulfilled in his person (cf. Luke 11:20). They lived in communion of life with Jesus who instructed them with his teaching, leaving them a new rule of life, by which they would be recognised as his disciples after his death (cf. John 13:34-35). By faith, they went out to the whole world, following the command to bring the Gospel to all creation (cf. Mark 16:15) and they fearlessly proclaimed to all the joy of the resurrection, of which they were faithful witnesses.' (Porta Fidei, 13)

These words from the Holy Father's apostolic letter announcing the Year of Faith are both a challenge and an encouragement to us all today. As the early Church bore faithful witness so are we called; as the early Church lived in communion with Christ and each other so are we called. Living a life of faith and witnessing to Christ is his wish for each of us.

The six group sessions of this booklet offer the opportunity to reflect on the twin realities of faith and mission which Christ entrusts to the Church and to each of us in baptism. It follows a similar format to previous *exploringfaith* resources [issuu. com/exploringfaith/docs] and draws its title from Blessed John Henry Newman's powerful prayer of the same name which can be found on the back cover.

The group sessions are supplemented by additional materials and text boxes on the themes as well as practical suggestions on sharing your faith and an opportunity to reflect further on your own faith journey. The booklet is illustrated with images which may serve to stir a thought in a way that the text may not. We also invite you to make use of the daily prayers in the second half of the booklet which are drawn from the Divine Office.

Each group session is written to last around one and a quarter hours but feel free to adapt the sessions as benefits your group.

This booklet is not tied to a particular time of year and the prayers and meditations may be used by individuals, groups or in a wider parish context at any time. In this Year of Faith, please do encourage others to join your group and to participate in the sharing of faith.

Three images at foot of page 5, L to R:
The Miraculous Draught of Fishes (by Jacopo Bassano - 1545), The Baptism of the Eunuch (by Rembrandt van Rijn -1641) and Jesus Washing Peter's Feet (by Ford Madox Brown -1876)

A Precious Treasure

Opening Prayers
Taken from Psalm 103(104)

Leader: Bless the Lord, my soul!
Lord God, how great you are,
clothed in majesty and glory,
wrapped in light as in a robe!

Group: How many are your works, O Lord!
In wisdom you have made them all.
The earth is full of your riches.

Leader: You hide your face, they are dismayed;
you take back your spirit, they die,
returning to the dust from which they came.

Group: You send forth your spirit, they are created;
and you renew the face of the earth.

Leader: May the glory of the Lord last for ever!
May the Lord rejoice in his works!

Group: May my thoughts be pleasing to him.
I find my joy in the Lord.

All: Glory be to the Father, and to the Son and to the Holy Spirit. As it was in
the beginning, is now, and ever shall be, world without end. Amen.

*As we come together let us, either aloud or in the silence of our hearts, give thanks
and praise to the Lord for all the things we have accomplished, the joys experienced,
graces received and people met over the past week. Let us also remember all those in
need of our prayers.*

Introduction to the Scripture reading
Let us listen carefully to the Word of the Lord,
and attend to it with the ear of our hearts.
Let us welcome it, and faithfully put it into practice.

St. Benedict of Nursia (c.480-c.547) adapte

Explore the Scriptures Ephesians 2:4-10

Note: Ephesians is one of the four Captivity Epistles, along with Philippians, Colossians, and Philemon. The letter was probably written from St Paul's imprisonment in Rome in 62-63 AD. This Letter is most noted for its description of Christ and the Church. In it Paul speaks of the Father's Plan for Salvation (Ephesians 1:3-6); the Church as the Body of Christ (1:22-23); and he calls for the exemplary living of the Church's members (4:1-5:5) to live as children of the light (5:8-5:20). Finally in the letter's most famous passage, Paul compares the relationship of Christ and the Church to the marriage relationship of husband and wife (Ephesians 5:21-33).

God, who is rich in mercy, out of the great love with which he loved us even when we were dead through our trespasses, made us alive together with Christ - by grace you have been saved - and raised us up with him and seated us with him in the heavenly places in Christ Jesus, so that in the ages to come he might show the immeasurable riches of his grace in kindness towards us in Christ Jesus. For by grace you have been saved through faith, and this is not your own doing; it is the gift of God - not the result of works, so that no one may boast. For we are what he has made us, created in Christ Jesus for good works, which God prepared beforehand to be our way of life.

Please take a few moments in silence to reflect on the passage, then share a word or phrase that has struck you. Pause to think about what others have said then, after a second reading of the passage, you may wish to share a further thought.

Reflection

Some gifts are lovingly cared for and enjoy pride of place in our homes; the giver cherished in our hearts. Others are set aside only to find their way to the top shelf of the closet, as we quickly forget who gave them. Take, for example, that attractive artistic item bought for you by a close friend or family member who knows your tastes – you would take the time to dust it, glancing at it from time to

L to R: *Parable of the Sower (by Vincent Van Gogh - 1888), Parable of the Yeast (by James Janknegt - 2003) and Parable of the Pearl (by Domenico Fetti - c.1610)*

time, perhaps smiling at a memory of time spent with its giver. Contrast this with the gift of a token or voucher where the gesture and even the initial gratitude can be lost in the lack of connection between the giver and the recipient, where it can be left in a wallet or drawer for months on end. It's often the thought of the giver that counts when it comes to receiver attaching value to the gift.

In Matthew's account of the gospel, in amongst various parables: the sower, the yeast and the mustard seed, Jesus gives us the extreme example of someone searching for something of great value. When he finds it, a remarkable and valuable pearl hidden in a field, he is not deterred by the cost but immediately sells all he owns to buy the field with the pearl in it. The message is clear – the value of the Kingdom is beyond obvious earthly wealth, the value of faith and wisdom is to be more esteemed than silver and gold (cf. Proverbs 16:16, Acts 17:11). In no way can it be said that we 'buy faith' – it is a gift gratuitously given by God – but the value we place on it is decided by us.

At baptism, when invited to say what they ask of the Church, the parents and godparents of the infant – or in the case of adults, on their own behalf – respond with a request for 'Faith'. They ask the Church that the seed of Faith be planted in their hearts in order that it might grow. Surrounded by the Christian community they seek its help on the journey to eternal life. In the same breath they are offering their own help to others, as we all seek to deepen our personal relationship with God the Father, Son and Spirit as hope-filled Children of God.

Faith, one of the theological virtues, is freely given – it is ours to accept or decline (*Catechism of the Catholic Church*, 1813). We may choose to cherish it, strengthen it and share it or we may choose to let it languish like the gift voucher in the drawer and the connection lost between the giver and the recipient.

Blessed John Henry Newman (1801-1890)
Originally an evangelical Oxford academic and Anglican priest, Newman left the Church of England in 1845 and was received into the Roman Catholic Church where he was eventually granted the rank of cardinal by Pope Leo XIII. He was instrumental in the founding of the Catholic University of Ireland, and is a literary figure of note. His major writings including his autobiography *Apologia Pro Vita Sua* (1865–66), the *Grammar of Assent* (1870), and the poem *The Dream of Gerontius* (1865), which was set to music by Edward Elgar. He also wrote the hymns 'Lead, Kindly Light' and 'Praise to the Holiest in the Height'. Newman's beatification was officially proclaimed by Pope Benedict XVI on 19 September 2010 during his visit to the United Kingdom.

A Precious Treasure **Radiating Christ**

Has the concept of gift been devalued in today's often 'quick and easy' world? How much thought do we give to the gifts we have actually been given rather than those we want? Do we recognise the importance of the gift of faith in our lives and give it the pride of place it deserves?

Closing Prayers

You may wish to end this session with some different prayers, silent reflection or Newman's 'Radiating Christ' which can be found on the back cover.

Lord, let me see your face,
know your heart
and experience your love in my life.
Strengthen in me the precious gift of faith.
I believe Lord;
Help my unbelief.
Amen.

Westminster Diocesan prayer for the Year of Faith (2012-2013)

Radiating Christ: What does my faith mean to me?

Ola - 'It gives meaning to my life, especially as a person discerning where I am going. I think it's difficult when you are young in today's world... I live abroad so I don't have my family or friends around me, so I am totally reliant on God and through that my faith has strengthened a lot... But it's not easy.'

Margaret - 'My faith actually means everything. It affects my whole life, it's the way my life is lived. It is to do with where we come from and where we are going to.'

Siobhan - 'There was a time when I wanted to walk away from God in my younger days and I found that I can't. I had to search... It is tied up with who I am, purpose, direction, focus and it gives me great hope. It's not escapism, it is the opposite... It roots me in reality.

Listen to more of the testimonies above at: https://vimeo.com/catholicism

Signpost

This session explored the idea of treasuring what we receive and in particular the precious gift of faith. Next session we will look at faith itself as something handed down over the centuries. Indeed, we will also look at our own part in this shared heritage. Before the next session you may wish to read articles 176-184 in the *Catechism*.

What is Faith?

Opening Prayers

Taken from St Paul's letter to the Ephesians 4:1-15

Leader: Lord, we humbly ask that we be made worthy
of the life to which you have called us,
grant us humility and gentleness,
help us to bear with one another in love,
making every effort to maintain
the unity of the Spirit in the bond of peace.

Group: There is one body and one Spirit,
there is one Lord, one faith, one baptism,
one God and Father of all,
who is above all and through all and in all.

Leader: Each of us was given grace
according to the measure of Christ's gift.

Group: The gifts he gave were that some would be apostles,
some prophets, some evangelists,
some pastors and teachers,
to equip the saints for the work of ministry,
for building up the body of Christ,

Leader: until all of us come to the unity of the faith
and of the knowledge of the Son of God,
to maturity, to the measure of the full stature of Christ.

Group: Grant that we no longer be children,
but speaking the truth in love,
may we grow up in every way into him
who is the head, into Christ. Amen.

As we come together let us, either aloud or in the silence of our hearts, give thanks and praise to the Lord for all the things we have accomplished, the joys experienced, graces received and people met over the past week. Let us also remember all those in need of our prayers.

Introduction to Reading of Scripture

Let us listen carefully to the Word of the Lord,
and attend to it with the ear of our hearts.
Let us welcome it, and faithfully put it into practice.

St. Benedict of Nursia (c.480-c.547) adapted

Explore the Scriptures Luke 2:39-52

Note: This passage is part of the 'hidden life' of Jesus' childhood. There are several childhood stories in what are known as the protoevangelia but not in the official canon of Scripture. After this glimpse of Jesus as a twelve year old we hear nothing more until his baptism at the hands of John the Baptist when he was around thirty years old.

When they had finished everything required by the law of the Lord, they returned to Galilee, to their own town of Nazareth. The child grew and became strong, filled with wisdom; and the favour of God was upon him.

Now every year his parents went to Jerusalem for the festival of the Passover. And when he was twelve years old, they went up as usual for the festival. When the festival was ended and they started to return, the boy Jesus stayed behind in Jerusalem, but his parents did not know it. Assuming that he was in the group of travellers, they went a day's journey. Then they started to look for him among their relatives and friends. When they did not find him, they returned to Jerusalem to search for him. After three days they found him in the temple, sitting among the teachers, listening to them and asking them questions. And all who heard him were amazed at his understanding and his answers. When his parents saw him they were astonished; and his mother said to him, 'Child, why have you treated us like this? Look, your father and I have been searching for you in great anxiety.' He said to them, 'Why were you searching for me? Did you not know that I must be in my Father's house?' But they did not understand what he said to them. Then he went down with them and came to Nazareth, and was obedient to them. His mother treasured all these things in her heart.

And Jesus increased in wisdom and in years, and in divine and human favour.

Please take a few moments in silence to reflect on the passage, then share a word or phrase that has struck you. Pause to think about what others have said then after a second reading of the passage you may wish to share a further thought.

Reflection

Who do you think you are?', a popular BBC/HBO television series has brought to the screen a remarkable number of fascinating stories. Each episode traces the family history of a celebrity and helps them to uncover their roots. Whether it is the Mayor of London exploring the life of his great-grandfather, a journalist killed in the Turkish war of independence, or the unexpected discoveries of Anglo-Indian roots by British comedian Alistair McGowan, to name but two, these stories enchant and fascinate.

Yet, while genealogists sift through computer generated databases and even DNA testing results to uncover blood relations and family anecdotes, our past can also be readily found in other sources. Holy Scripture sheds light on centuries of our shared ancestral history and clearly sets out the family relationship that we have rooted in our being 'adopted brothers and sisters in Christ'.

One thousand eight hundred years before the birth of Christ lived Abraham, who St Paul calls 'the father of all who believe' (Romans 4:11). What marked Abraham as a man of faith – what the *Catechism* describes as 'a supernatural gift' (CCC, 179) – was his ability to accept the divine invitation rather than to reject it. Abraham chose to look beyond the tangible and to trust in the Lord. Indeed, the very essence of faith is the ability to trust and hope in God, creator of the visible and invisible. Faith, as the Letter to the Hebrews defines, is 'the assurance of things hoped for, the conviction of things not seen' (Hebrews 11:1).

Down through the ages, Abraham's descendants – Elijah, King David and John the Baptist, among others – proclaimed God's desire that humankind should have the promise of eternal life. Responding to this gift – the hope of salvation – they grew in number as a people united in faith. While patiently waiting for the promised Saviour, they accepted that which the Lord revealed even when it seemed beyond human comprehension. Yet, God, our Father did not intend these revelations about himself to be accepted blindly. On contrary, as the *Catechism* explains: 'In faith, the human intellect and will co-operate with divine grace' (CCC, 155).

L to R: Abraham Journey from Ur to Canaan (by József Molnár), Elijah in the Wilderness (by Frederick Leighton) and King David between Wisdom and Prophecy (Paris Psalter)

What is Faith? **Radiating Christ**

ust as the Jewish people sought understanding in the teachings of Old Testament priests, kings and prophets; we too are invited to contemplate our family heritage (see also pages 56-57). In our contemplation of the treasure that comprises the Church's sacred Tradition, Holy Scripture as well as the lives of the saints we not only discover the story of our salvation handed on by those who have gone before us but also reflect on its impact in our lives today and our capacity for faith-filled growth in years yet to come.

What place does the reading of Scripture play in my daily routine? Who has impacted on my journey of faith and how? Who have I helped and how (see also page 62)? How do I see my place in the story of salvation?

Closing Prayers
You may wish to end this session with some different prayers, silent reflection or Newman's 'Radiating Christ' which can be found on the back cover.

Lord, let me see your face,
know your heart
and experience your love in my life.
Strengthen in me the precious gift of faith.
I believe Lord;
Help my unbelief.
Amen.

Westminster Diocesan prayer for the Year of Faith (2012-2013)

Radiating Christ: What does my faith mean to me?

Veronica - 'Faith really is at the heart of my life. I would describe it as the fabric of my being. It's an ongoing journey and an ongoing adventure. There have been many phases to it when I reflect and look back, but there has been a solid core. I can remember as a child learning that faith is a gift of God and I think now as I'm getting a little bit older, I'm really beginning to appreciate the truth of that; to recognise that actually I've been very blessed with the gift of faith throughout my life. That has manifest itself really in friends and family who have shared their faith with me. I've been very fortunate in meeting some remarkable people and have had some amazing opportunities to develop my faith, and for that I'm very very grateful.'

Listen to more of the testimonies above at: https://vimeo.com/catholicism

Signpost

This session looked at the bonds of faith we share, with our Jewish cousins and each other, and the assent of both mind and heart to God's invitation. Next session will look at the person of Jesus of Nazareth, the anointed one of God, who transformed the world. Before the next session have a look at articles 452-455 and 479-483 in the *Catechism*.

Not What but Who

Opening prayer
Taken from Isaiah 61:1-3, 10-11

Leader: The spirit of the Lord God is upon me,
because the Lord has anointed me;
he has sent me to bring good news to the oppressed,
to bind up the broken-hearted,

Group: to proclaim liberty to the captives,
and release to the prisoners;
to proclaim the year of the Lord's favour,
and the day of vengeance of our God;
to comfort all who mourn;

Leader: to give them a garland instead of ashes,
the oil of gladness instead of mourning,
the mantle of praise instead of a faint spirit.

Group: I will greatly rejoice in the Lord,
my whole being shall exult in my God;
for he has clothed me with the garments of salvation,
he has covered me with the robe of righteousness,
as a bridegroom decks himself with a garland,
and as a bride adorns herself with her jewels.

Leader: For as the earth brings forth its shoots,
and as a garden causes what is sown in it to spring up,
so the Lord God will cause righteousness and praise
to spring up before all the nations.

All: Glory be to the Father, and to the Son and to the Holy Spirit. As it was in
the beginning, is now, and ever shall be, world without end. Amen.

*As we come together let us, either aloud or in the silence of our hearts, give thanks
and praise to the Lord for all the things we have accomplished, the joys experienced,
graces received and people met over the past week. Let us also remember all those in
need of our prayers.*

Introduction to Reading of Scripture

Let us listen carefully to the Word of the Lord,
and attend to it with the ear of our hearts.
Let us welcome it, and faithfully put it into practice.

St. Benedict of Nursia (c.480-c.547) adapted

Explore the Scriptures Mark 8:27-35

Note: Immediately prior to this episode, before setting off for Caesarea Philippi, Jesus had cured a blind man at Bethsaida. Six days later, Peter, James and John were to experience the wonder of Jesus' transfiguration on Mount Tabor (an event remembered with joy by Peter in his second letter addressed to 'all who treasure the same faith as ourselves, given through the righteousness of our God and saviour Jesus Christ' – 2 Peter 1:16-18).

Jesus went on with his disciples to the villages of Caesarea Philippi; and on the way he asked his disciples, 'Who do people say that I am?' And they answered him 'John the Baptist; and others, Elijah; and still others, one of the prophets.' He asked them, 'But who do you say that I am?' Peter answered him, 'You are the Messiah.' And he sternly ordered them not to tell anyone about him.

Then he began to teach them that the Son of Man must undergo great suffering, and be rejected by the elders, the chief priests, and the scribes, and be killed, and after three days rise again. He said all this quite openly. And Peter took him aside and began to rebuke him. But turning and looking at his disciples, he rebuked Peter and said, 'Get behind me, Satan! For you are setting your mind not on divine things but on human things.'

He called the crowd with his disciples, and said to them, 'If any want to become my followers, let them deny themselves and take up their cross and follow me. For those who want to save their life will lose it, and those who lose their life for my sake, and for the sake of the gospel, will save it.

Please take a few moments in silence to reflect on the passage, then share a word or phrase that has struck you. Pause to think about what others have said then after a second reading of the passage you may wish to share a further thought.

Reflection

Much has been made of the danger and superficiality of celebrity and particularly the worship of celebrity. From mirroring Victoria Beckham's fashion sense to Justin Beiber's huge twitter following, the devotion which celebrities attract from their 'followers' is tremendous. Witness also, the groundswell of support for sportspeople like Andy Murray who made but lost the Wimbledon final in 2012 or Jody Cundy in the Paralympic cycling who was harshly disqualified. Such close identifying of oneself with another allows something of a share in their joy but can lead to a sense of disappointment whenever the ideal is compromised or the goal left unaccomplished.

Not What but Who **Radiating Christ**

n his book *Confessions*, St Augustine of Hippo famously addresses God saying: 'You arouse us so that praising you may bring us joy, because you have made us and drawn us to yourself, and our heart is unquiet until it rests in you,' or, in another translation, 'you have made us for yourself, O Lord, and our heart is restless until it rests in you.' The culture of celebrity can be seen as an example of this restlessness. The love we have for family and friends too, while precious, can be seen as but a taste, an imperfect solution to the deepest yearning we feel as we search for God.

In Jesus, God the Son, we have the perfect role model for human living; in him we have the answer to these yearnings and the sure path to the loving embrace of the God the Father. Each of us is required to recognise Christ's role in the redemption of humanity and our own personal salvation, each of us is needed to confess, like Peter, 'You are the Christ, the son of the living God'. Jesus did not tell Peter what to say but simply asked the question – who do you say I am? Who am I to you? The same question is ours to answer.

It was through faith that Peter grasped who Jesus truly was. He was the first apostle to recognise Jesus as the Christ (the Anointed One or Messiah) and he along with the others were tasked with sharing this revelation to the world (Matthew 28:19). Communicating to others who Jesus is would be impossible without knowing him for ourselves, without understanding with both head and heart what God has done in Jesus for us all. Jesus is the cornerstone of our faith, the keystone which the builders had rejected (Psalm 118:22, Acts 4:11). It is through our response to God's freely given grace that we understand Jesus as the centre of our faith and recognise the gift of himself in the Eucharist. It is through baptism that we share in his anointing and mission to the world. Being a Christian, is being Christ to others and entering a loving relationship with him with our whole self. Should anyone ask what we believe as Christians, let our response not be about what we believe but about the one in whom we believe.

Our privilage and our duty

'At the heart of catechesis we find, in essence, a Person, the Person of Jesus of Nazareth, the only Son from the Father. . .who suffered and died for us and who now, after rising, is living with us forever.' To catechise is 'to reveal in the Person of Christ the whole of God's eternal design reaching fulfillment in that Person. It is to seek to understand the meaning of Christ's actions and words and of the signs worked by him.' Catechesis aims at putting 'people . . . in communion . . . with Jesus Christ: only he can lead us to the love of the Father in the Spirit and make us share in the life of the Holy Trinity' (*Catechism*, 426).

Who is Jesus to me... just a good man, a teacher, the Son of God? What impact does realising who Jesus really is have on us? Is it possible to live up to Jesus' message and follow his example in the twenty-first century?

Closing Prayers
You may wish to end this session with some different prayers, silent reflection or Newman' 'Radiating Christ' which can be found on the back cover.

Lord Jesus Christ,
the Way, the Truth, and the Life;
let us not stray from you, the Way,
nor distrust you, the Truth,
nor rest in any other but you, the Life;
teach us by your Holy Spirit who to believe,
what to do,
and in what to take our rest;
we ask it for your name's sake.
Amen.

Radiating Christ: What does my faith mean to me?

Fr Gareth - 'When I was a teenager I read the gospel seriously for the first time. I discovered that this Jesus was quite demanding actually. He said, 'if you are going to follow me, don't turn back once you've put your hand to the plough, it's going to be difficult, but there are going to be great rewards,' and this had a ring of truth about it. So faith to me now is having a quiet inner confidence that the hard work and loving of other people, which is what Jesus asks of me, is worthwhile. When I get to the end of my life, I'm looking forward to that "well done good and faithful servant"... When Jesus said "do this in memory of me" and then "love other people as I have loved you," that really resonates with me. I know deep down that if I live life that way, when I get to the end of my life, it is going to be good.'

Listen to more of the testimonies above at: https://vimeo.com/catholicism

Signpost

This session looked at Jesus Christ, the Son of God, as the model for perfect living. Our faith is not a list to be ticked off but a relationship with Jesus who is the Way, the Truth and the Life. Next session we will explore our loving response to the love God has shown us. Before the next session have a look at articles 1833-1845 in the *Catechism*.

Icon of Jesus Christ as the True Vine by an anonymous Greek icon writer (16th century)

Responding in Love

Opening prayer
Taken from Psalm 111(112)

Leader: Praise the Lord!
Happy are those who fear the Lord,
who greatly delight in his commandments.

Group: Their descendants will be mighty in the land;
the generation of the upright will be blessed.
Wealth and riches are in their houses,
and their righteousness endures for ever.

Leader: They rise in the darkness as a light for the upright;
they are gracious, merciful, and righteous.
It is well with those who deal generously and lend,
who conduct their affairs with justice.

Group: For the righteous will never be moved;
they will be remembered for ever.
They are not afraid of evil tidings;
their hearts are firm, secure in the Lord.

Leader: Their hearts are steady, they will not be afraid;
in the end they will look in triumph on their foes.

Group: They have distributed freely, they have given to the poor;
their righteousness endures for ever;
their heads are raised in glory.

All: Glory be to the Father, and to the Son and to the Holy Spirit. As it was in
the beginning, is now, and ever shall be, world without end. Amen.

*As we come together let us, either aloud or in the silence of our hearts, give thanks
and praise to the Lord for all the things we have accomplished, the joys experienced,
graces received and people met over the past week. Let us also remember all those in
need of our prayers.*

Introduction to Reading of Scripture

Let us pray with great confidence, with confidence based upon the goodness and infinite generosity of God and upon the promises of Jesus Christ. God is a spring of living water which flows unceasingly into the hearts of those who pray.

St Louis de Montfort (1673-1716)

Explore the Scriptures John 15:4-5, 9-17

Note: John's gospel, so rich in symbolism, here recounts what we refer to as Jesus' farewell discourses. After washing his disciples' feet Jesus explains what will come to pass in his Passion, Death and Resurrection and the coming of the Holy Spirit. Not long after this long passage, in which he describes himself as the 'True Vine', he is arrested in the Garden of Gethsemane.

'Abide in me as I abide in you. Just as the branch cannot bear fruit by itself unless it abides in the vine, neither can you unless you abide in me. I am the vine, you are the branches. Those who abide in me and I in them bear much fruit, because apart from me you can do nothing.'

'As the Father has loved me, so I have loved you; abide in my love. If you keep my commandments, you will abide in my love, just as I have kept my Father's commandments and abide in his love. I have said these things to you so that my joy may be in you, and that your joy may be complete.

'This is my commandment, that you love one another as I have loved you. No one has greater love than this, to lay down one's life for one's friends. You are my friends if you do what I command you. I do not call you servants any longer, because the servant does not know what the master is doing; but I have called you friends, because I have made known to you everything that I have heard from my Father. You did not choose me but I chose you. And I appointed you to go and bear fruit, fruit that will last, so that the Father will give you whatever you ask him in my name. I am giving you these commands so that you may love one another.'

Please take a few moments in silence to reflect on the passage, then share a word or phrase that has struck you. Pause to think about what others have said then after a second reading of the passage you may wish to share a further thought.

Reflection

Some years ago a story ran asking people whether the Cross should be replaced as the symbol of Christianity with something 'a little less depressing'. It was suggested that as the Cross is an instrument of torture and painful humiliating death, it should be replaced with something like an image of the empty tomb or a chick symbolising new life.

The Cross, however, has to be seen in a rather different light. Yes, it was the place where our Lord suffered pain, thirst and anguish and where 'he bowed his head and gave up his spirit' (John 19:30), but it is also the place where we most vividly see the love of God. On the Cross we see the love of Jesus for us in his obedience to the Father, 'even to accepting death, death on a Cross' (Philippians 2:8) and the love of the Father in offering his own son 'for us and our salvation' (Nicene Creed).

It is perfectly possible to see, in this light, the excruciating death that Christ suffered as a loving act. When we consider what a parent would go through for a child, or a friend for a friend, love in suffering is not as strange as it first may seem. Such love as Jesus showed, the Holy Father wrote in *Caritas in Veritate*, 'is God's greatest gift to humanity, it is his promise and our hope' (CIV, 2).

Through the Year of Faith we have the opportunity to get to know Christ better, he who invites us to share in his life and mission; he who suffers for and with us; he who shows us compassion and love and he who guides us in prayer and contemplation. Each of these facets of his life was perfectly integrated and the invitation is there for us to resist living our lives in bits and pieces and yield to his pattern, his way of living.

Rarely is Jesus' consistent witness better shown than in his answer to the Pharisee when asked 'which commandment in the law is the greatest?' (Matthew 22:36-40). Narrowing the 613 mitzvot (laws) observed by his fellow Jews, reducing down even the Ten Commandments to just two, Jesus gives us all a clear instruction to love God and love neighbour. In loving God, through worship and praise, we give him pride of place in our lives, thanking him for that act of perfect love that reconciled us to him. In loving neighbour, through acts of genuine caritas we come to see the face of Christ in all we meet (Matthew 25:40, see also Psalm 26(27):7-9).

In loving God joyfully through our devotions and prayer and in loving neighbour generously, we give witness to God's glory and his love for humanity. It is not a question of telling people what they should believe; it's more a question of living

Responding in Love **Radiating Christ**

that belief for them to see. Certainly we may be asked to justify ourselves (1 Peter 3:15 and Mark 13:9-11) but witness is more powerful than instructing. Proposing Christ as a way of life is more powerful than imposing our position. Gently but firmly offering the gift of faith, truth and life was the way of the Lord (e.g. John 4:1-42); so it can and should be for us.

What opportunities have I had to talk about my faith? Where has the way someone behaved made me think about how I live my own life? How do I seek to live out my Christian faith and how can I strengthen my witness to Christ?

Closing Prayers

You may wish to end this session with some different prayers, silent reflection or Newman's 'Radiating Christ' which can be found on the back cover.

God grant me the serenity to accept the things I cannot change;
courage to change the things I can;
and wisdom to know the difference.
Living one day at a time;
enjoying one moment at a time;
accepting hardships as the pathway to peace;
taking, as He did, this sinful world as it is, not as I would have it;
trusting that He will make all things right if I surrender to His Will;
that I may be reasonably happy in this life
and supremely happy with Him forever in the next.
Amen.

The Serenity Prayer (c. 1942) by Reinhold Niebuhr (1892-1971)

Radiating Christ: What does my faith mean to me?

Uje - 'My faith is an integral part of my life. For me it is sort of a compass, or even a central point around which most things in my life rotate. It gives me a sense of direction and it gives me a sense of belonging. It connects me to God Almighty, who I know is in control of everything... at least I know that I'm not in control of my life and that gives me so much relief that I don't have to control the things around my life. It is really, for me, about the Communion of Saints as well, to know that at every point in time, no matter how alone I might find myself to be, I am always within the Communion of Saints' (see the *Catechism of the Catholic Church* 960-962).

Listen to more of the testimonies above at: https://vimeo.com/catholicism

Signpost This session looked at caritas and the way we are called to live as followers of Christ. Together prayer and loving action form the bedrock of our discipleship. Next session we will look at how the Church nurtures and matures our faith. Before the next session you may wish to read articles 802-810 and 866-870 in the *Catechism*.

A Place to Grow Together

Opening prayer

The Nicene Creed, composed in part and adopted at the First Council of Nicaea (AD325) and revised with additions by the First Council of Constantinople (AD381) is also known as the Symbol of Faith.

All: I believe in one God,
the Father almighty,
maker of heaven and earth,
of all things visible and invisible.
I believe in one Lord Jesus Christ,
the Only Begotten Son of God,
born of the Father before all ages.
God from God, Light from Light,
true God from true God,
begotten, not made, consubstantial with the Father;
through him all things were made.
For us men and for our salvation
he came down from heaven,
and by the Holy Spirit was incarnate of the Virgin Mary,
and became man.
For our sake he was crucified under Pontius Pilate,
he suffered death and was buried,
and rose again on the third day
in accordance with the Scriptures.
He ascended into heaven
and is seated at the right hand of the Father.
He will come again in glory
to judge the living and the dead
and his kingdom will have no end.
I believe in the Holy Spirit, the Lord, the giver of life,
who proceeds from the Father and the Son,
who with the Father and the Son is adored and glorified,
who has spoken through the prophets.
I believe in one, holy, catholic and apostolic Church.
I confess one baptism for the forgiveness of sins
and I look forward to the resurrection of the dead
and the life of the world to come.
Amen.

As we come together let us, either aloud or in the silence of our hearts, give thanks and praise to the Lord for all the things we have accomplished, the joys experienced, graces received and people met over the past week. Let us also remember all those in need of our prayers.

Introduction to Reading of Scripture

Let us go forward in peace, our eyes upon heaven, the only one goal of our labours.

St. Thérèse of Lisieux (1873-1897)

Explore the Scriptures Romans 15:1-9, 12-13

Note: The first letter by St Paul to appear in the Bible, his Letter to the Romans opens with a summary of essential Christian belief (1:1-4), and addresses the importance of the Gospel message for humanity (1:16-3:20). Paul recognises the eternal struggle in humanity between the spirit and the flesh (chapters 6-8) and the tension between the Greek and Jewish members of the Roman community. In this passage we read of the need for harmony for the sake of the Gospel.

We who are strong ought to put up with the failings of the weak, and not to please ourselves. Each of us must please our neighbour for the good purpose of building up the neighbour. For Christ did not please himself; but, as it is written, 'The insults of those who insult you have fallen on me.' For whatever was written in former days was written for our instruction, so that by steadfastness and by the encouragement of the scriptures we might have hope. May the God of steadfastness and encouragement grant you to live in harmony with one another, in accordance with Christ Jesus, so that together you may with one voice glorify the God and Father of our Lord Jesus Christ.

Welcome one another, therefore, just as Christ has welcomed you, for the glory of God. For I tell you that Christ has become a servant of the circumcised on behalf of the truth of God in order that he might confirm the promises given to the patriarchs, and in order that the Gentiles might glorify God for his mercy. As it is written:

'Therefore I will confess you among the Gentiles, and sing praises to your name'; and again Isaiah says,
'The root of Jesse shall come, the one who rises to rule the Gentiles; in him the Gentiles shall hope.'

May the God of hope fill you with all joy and peace in believing, so that you may abound in hope by the power of the Holy Spirit.

Please take a few moments in silence to reflect on the passage, then share a word or phrase that has struck you. Pause to think about what others have said then after a second reading of the passage you may wish to share a further thought.

Reflection

Some of us might recall with fondness a famous 1970s television programme called *The Waltons*, in which the main character was John Boy, the eldest son. In each programme a story would be shared of how a lesson had been learnt in love and understanding. What the programme powerfully affirmed was that the family is a place of learning and growth. Whether we enjoyed a conventional family upbringing or not, everyone takes the childhood lessons they learn in the family into adult life.

The Catholic Church is also essentially a family. Made up of people from a diverse range of backgrounds, together with those who have gone before us marked with the sign of faith, the Church makes up the Body of Christ (Colossians 1:24). Through baptism these people, who might otherwise be strangers, aim to live in deep spiritual communion with one another, sustained by the Eucharist and the Sacramental life of the Church. In this family of the Church, expressed and experienced locally in the parish, we learn to love and grow in faith. We learn to forgive and be forgiven having been given the grace to do so by the Holy Spirit, the Spirit present in each person and in the whole body of the Church.

At Pentecost we witness the birth of the Church in the Upper Room. The Apostles and Our Lady, having seen Christ after his Resurrection, are filled with the Holy Spirit and are compelled to proclaim the message of the Gospel of Jesus. It was a dramatic and amazing moment with three thousand people subsequently converted to the 'Christian' movement.

It is important to appreciate that the disciples didn't just stumble on this great moment of grace. They had spent three years being prepared for it, learning from Jesus and from their mistakes, to live and share his message. In a sense, although Pentecost day is celebrated as the birth of the Church, the disciples had been apprentices in building the Church (in Latin 'ecclesia' meaning 'assembly'), learning each day as they walked with Christ. Their little assembly, centred on Jesus, was where their weak faith was nurtured and tested, strengthened and matured so they were ready to respond when the Holy Spirit filled them in the Upper Room.

It is east to forget the purpose of the Church in our busy daily lives – at work, home and in parish life. Both universally and locally, in joys and challenges, the Church helps us to grow in faith, to practice charity and forgiveness and to evangelise. As we journey together – in our families, our parishes, our faith-sharing groups – opportunities arise for us to gain strength and to give witness to Christ.

A Place to Grow Together **Radiating Christ**

Faith is not received as a fully mature gift at baptism. It takes time to grow, which is why the Church is so essential to everyone's journey of faith. If we cut ourselves off from it we distance ourselves from the people and gifts that we need as we seek and find lasting happiness.

What joy do I find in my faith? How have I shared this with others? What have I done to nourish my relationship with Christ? How have I encouraged others in fulfilling their responsibility to grow in their faith?

Closing Prayers
You may wish to end this session with some different prayers, silent reflection or Newman's 'Radiating Christ' which can be found on the back cover.

Thank you Lord for the gift of faith,
help us to never take it for granted,
give us the grace to grow in faith everyday.
Send your Holy Spirit down upon us now,
so that as we prepare to leave this place,
we might, as did the Apostles at Pentecost,
be attentive to the opportunities that you give us,
to deepen our understanding of and to share this great treasure.
Amen.

Radiating Christ: What does my faith mean to me?

Sr Nuala - 'My faith... it's like the air I breathe. It is life. It is rooted in my personal relationship with Jesus Christ, giving purpose and meaning to everything.'

Bruce - 'My faith is everything to me. I can't imagine myself without it really. The thing that nourishes me and kept me through good and bad times is my devotion to the Eucharist, which is central to me.'

Listen to more of the testimonies above at: https://vimeo.com/catholicism

Signpost

This session looked at the Church as a family in which we prepare and live as apprentices to Christ in love. The next and final session of this booklet will explore how the Church as a whole and we as individuals are called to spread the Good News of Jesus. Before the next session you may wish to read articles 905, 1072 and 425 in the *Catechism*.

The Sharing of the Gift

Opening prayer
Taken from Psalm 26(27)

Leader: The Lord is my light and my help;
whom shall I fear?
The Lord is the stronghold of my life;
before whom shall I shrink?

Group: Though an army encamp against me
my heart would not fear.
Though war break out against me
even then would I trust.

Leader: And now my head shall be raised
above my foes who surround me
and I shall offer within his tent
a sacrifice of joy.

Group: May the glory of the Lord endure for ever;
may the Lord rejoice in his works -
I will sing to the Lord as long as I live;
I will sing praise to my God while I have being.

Leader: O Lord, hear my voice when I call;
have mercy and answer.
Of you my heart has spoken: 'Seek his face.'
It is your face, O Lord, that I seek; hide not your face.

All: Glory be to the Father, and to the Son and to the Holy Spirit. As it was in
the beginning, is now, and ever shall be, world without end. Amen.

*As we come together let us, either aloud or in the silence of our hearts, give thanks
and praise to the Lord for all the things we have accomplished, the joys experienced,
graces received and people met over the past week. Let us also remember all those in
need of our prayers.*

Introduction to Reading of Scripture
Christ be with me, Christ within me, Christ behind me, Christ before me, Christ
beside me, Christ to win me, Christ to comfort me and restore me.

attributed to St. Patrick (c.387 – 493 or c.460)

Explore the Scriptures James 1:17-27

Note: The Letter of James is the first of seven universal letters of the New Testament, so called because they are addressed to the universal Church in general and not to a specific community, e.g. the Philippians. It is a highly important work because of the key concept of the necessity of works along with faith in chapter two as well as the various encouragements to live God's word, to be impartial, to control the tongue, and its talk of the danger of worldliness and wealth. Chapter 5:13-15 serves as the foundation for the Sacrament of the Anointing of the Sick.

Every generous act of giving, with every perfect gift, is from above, coming down from the Father of lights, with whom there is no variation or shadow due to change. In fulfilment of his own purpose he gave us birth by the word of truth, so that we would become a kind of first fruits of his creatures.

You must understand this, my beloved: let everyone be quick to listen, slow to speak, slow to anger; for your anger does not produce God's righteousness. Therefore rid yourselves of all sordidness and rank growth of wickedness, and welcome with meekness the implanted word that has the power to save your souls.

But be doers of the word, and not merely hearers who deceive themselves. For if any are hearers of the word and not doers, they are like those who look at themselves in a mirror; for they look at themselves and, on going away, immediately forget what they were like. But those who look into the perfect law, the law of liberty, and persevere, being not hearers who forget but doers who act - they will be blessed in their doing.

If any think they are religious, and do not bridle their tongues but deceive their hearts, their religion is worthless. Religion that is pure and undefiled before God, the Father, is this: to care for orphans and widows in their distress, and to keep oneself unstained by the world.

Please take a few moments in silence to reflect on the passage, then share a word or phrase that has struck you. Pause to think about what others have said then after a second reading of the passage you may wish to share a further thought.

Reflection

One of the most famous written works by saint and martyr, Thomas More, was published in 1516 titled *Utopia*. He used it to describe a fictional island in the Atlantic Ocean where there is communal ownership of land, private property does not exist, men and women are educated alike, and there is almost complete religious toleration. The same word is used today to refer to communities that attempt to create an ideal society. There is much in St Thomas's description of Utopia that is reminiscent of the description of the early Christian community in the Acts of the Apostles (2:42-47).

Striking in the witness of the early Church community is the simplicity of its shared lifestyle, which stands in contrast to our often-complicated daily lives. These first Christians, filled with the joy of the Holy Spirit, shared what they had. Everything was owned in common and they even sold their possessions to serve those in need. Alongside this, they didn't neglect their spiritual practices and regularly went to the Temple, also meeting in each other's houses to break bread and share the food that they had. It is wonderful to read that they did this 'gladly and generously', praising God. Through the observance of these simple and yet radical actions, people noticed them and as a result sought to join them.

There were certainly tensions in the Early Christian community (e.g. Acts 15) but how they lived and loved inspired comment (John 13:35) and poses a real challenge to us today. Their example asks us to reflect very closely on the witness of our local Christian communities and schools. It prompts reflection about how effectively, as individuals and as local Christian communities, we radiate Christ and 'are looked up to' by those within and outside of our family of faith. It surely causes each of us to ask how selfless, joy-filled and radical we are in making the mercy and love of Christ present to others, through both word and action.

There are so many people we meet and know who are searching for meaning. They might not put it in those terms, but they are trying to fill gaps and run from the brokenness of their lives. It is our duty, as we read in *Evangelii Nuntiandi* (On Evangelisation in the Modern World), to reach out and witness to hope, in our own brokenness and weakness, through our prayers, words and actions (EN, 14). We are called to be beacons of light and hope (Matthew 5:15). The gift of our faith is not solely for ourselves. It is not a selfish thing to be put in our metaphorical box of treasures and brought out now and again for our own gratification. The dynamic of faith is that if it is not shared it dies (Matthew 13). In sharing the gift of faith we find that it grows and intensifies. Even when our efforts might seem to fall short or fail, we know and trust that every person is in God's loving hands.

Blessed John Henry Newman understood this calling and duty profoundly when he wrote his meditation *Radiating Christ*. He knew that in opening all that he was

Chinese Whispers by Diana Matthis

The Sharing of the Gift **Radiating Christ**

to the Holy Spirit, God would shine through him and bring others to the Lord's Light. He understood that in responding to the call to mission we achieve nothing solely through our own efforts, but are reliant on God's grace. We are empty vessels, called to stay close to Christ and to His Bride, the Church, called to be filled with faith. The vocation to mission involves using all the gifts that we've been given – using faith and reason, the heart and mind. In this we radiate the presence of Christ.

How do we witness to our faith in our everyday lives? What part does joy play in the living and sharing of our faith? What new thing have we learnt through this gathering about the ways in which we can radiate Christ?

Closing Prayers
You may wish to end this session with some different prayers, silent reflection or Newman's 'Radiating Christ' which can be found on the back cover.

As the seed grows silently in the earth,
as the yeast rises in the dough,
may your power, Spirit of God, be at work in us.
like a city set on a hill,
like a lamp shining in the darkness,
may we witness together,
calling our brothers and sisters to the glory of your light
and the peace and justice of your kingdom.
Amen.

Radiating Christ: What does my faith mean to me?

Davina - 'My faith means to me everything. It is something that I just thank God for every day. Whenever things go wrong, or things are really really difficult, that's when I just rely on it to get me through and it always does.'

Timothy - 'My faith, for me, means being brought up as a Catholic... it also means everything else that has happened to me, taking part in the life of the Church... in the services of the Church, the Mass, taking part in the liturgies as an organist and singer. It also means participating in other activities of the Church's mission such as justice and peace work and working for CAFOD. It is a very complete experience really and very central to my life.'

Listen to more of the testimonies above at: https://vimeo.com/catholicism

Signpost

This session explored the life of the Early Church and the example they provide us in giving Christian witness to the world at large. Each of us is called to use our gifts in the service of the gospel. The faith-sharing resource for Lent 2013 will be on reconciliation and mercy, a prominent theme for the Year of Faith (October 2012-November 2013)

The Four Evangelists by Jacob Jordaens (c.1625)

Radiating Christ

Daily Prayer
Sunday to Saturday

The daily prayers on the following pages are drawn from the Divine Office (Liturgy of the Hours). Each day contains a hymn, a Scripture reading, a psalm or canticle and a selection of prayers taken from the feasts of the four evangelists: St Mark (25 Apr), St Matthew (21 Sep), St Luke (18 Oct) and St John (27 Dec), as well as the Solemnities of Pentecost & The Birthday of St John the Baptist (24 June).

Together with the Mass, the Divine Office (Liturgy of the Hours) constitutes the official public prayer life of the Church. It is celebrated, under different names, in both the Eastern and Western Churches. The Divine Office is intended to be read communally but here we invite you to use it as a personal daily prayer.

'The Office is... the prayer not only of the clergy but of the whole People of God.'   *Apostolic Constitution, Canticum Laudis*

Sunday - Come, Holy Spirit

Introduction

O God, come to our aid. Lord, make haste to help us.

Glory be to the Father and to the Son and to the Holy Spirit, as it was in the beginning, is now, and ever shall be, world without end. Amen. (Alleluia)

omit Alleluias during Lent

Hymn

A mighty wind invades the world,
So strong and free on beating wing:
It is the Spirit of the Lord
From whom all truth and freedom spring.

The Spirit is a fountain clear
For ever leaping to the sky,
Whose waters give unending life,
Whose timeless source is never dry.

The Spirit comes in tongues of flame,
With love and wisdom burning bright,
The wind, the fountain and the fire
Combine in this great feast of light.

O tranquil Spirit, bring us peace,
With God the Father and the Son.
We praise you, blessed Trinity,
Unchanging, and for ever One.

Antiphon

The Holy Spirit, who comes from the Father, will glorify me, alleluia.

Psalmody

Psalm 112(113)

Praise, O servants of the Lord,
praise the name of the Lord!
May the name of the Lord be blessed
both now and for evermore!
From the rising of the sun to its setting
praised be the name of the Lord!

High above all nations is the Lord,
above the heavens his glory.
Who is like the Lord, our God,
who has risen on high to his throne
yet stoops from the heights to look down,
to look down upon heaven and earth?

From the dust he lifts up the lowly,
from the dungheap he raises the poor
to set them in the company of princes,
yes, with the princes of his people.
To the childless wife he gives a home
and gladdens her heart with children.

Glory be…

Antiphon

The Holy Spirit, who comes from the Father, will glorify me, alleluia.

Reading   *Ephesians 4:3-6*

Do your best to preserve the unity which the Spirit gives, by the peace that binds you together. There is one Body and one Spirit, just as there is one hope to which God has called you. There is one Lord, one faith, one baptism; there is one God and Father of all, who is Lord of all, works through all, and is in all.

Short Responsory
℟ The Holy Spirit is the Advocate.
℣ He will teach you everything.
Glory be…

Benedictus/Magnificat Antiphon
Come, Holy Spirit, fill the hearts of your faithful, and enkindle in them the fire of your love; though the peoples spoke different tongues you united them in proclaiming the same faith, alleluia.

Benedictus (if said in the morning)
or Magnificat (if said in the evening) -
see inside front cover for these prayers

Intercessions
The apostles waited and prayed for the coming of the Spirit. We too pray for his coming, and joyfully proclaim the greatness of God.
℟ Father, send us your Spirit.

In Christ you restored the universe which you had made; through the Spirit renew the face of the earth.
℟ Father, send us your Spirit.

You breathed into Adam the breath of life: breathe your Spirit into the Church, that the world may find life in her.
℟ Father, send us your Spirit.

May your Spirit bring light to our darkness; turn hatred into love, sorrow into joy, and doubt into hope. Cleanse and refresh us in the waters of the Spirit; where there is anguish and sin, bring healing and rebirth.
℟ Father, send us your Spirit.

Our Father…

Concluding prayer
Almighty, ever-living God,
you ordained that the paschal mystery
be completed by the mystery of
   Pentecost.
Gather together, by your gift of grace,
   the scattered nations and divided
   tongues
   to one faith in your Name.
Through Christ our Lord.
Amen.

Detail from *Cathedra Petri* (1647-53) by Gian Lorenzo Bernini in St Peter's Basilica, Rome

Radiating Christ

Monday - Matthew
the 'winged man': figure of reason

Introduction
O God, come to our aid. Lord, make haste to help us.

Glory be to the Father and to the Son and to the Holy Spirit, as it was in the beginning, is now, and ever shall be, world without end. Amen. (Alleluia)

omit Alleluias during Lent

Hymn
O fathers of our ancient faith,
with all the heav'ns we sing your fame
Whose sound went forth in all the earth
To tell of Christ, and bless his name.

You took the gospel to the poor,
The word of God alight in you,
Which in our day is told again:
That timeless word, for ever new.

You told of God who died for us
And out of death triumphant rose,
who gave the truth that made us free,
And changeless through the ages goes.

Praise Father, Son and Holy Ghost
Whose gift is faith that never dies:
A light in darkness now, until
The day-star in our hearts arise.

Stanbrook Abbey Hymnal

Antiphon
You are my friends since you have remained in my love.

Psalmody

Psalm 115 (116)

I trusted, even when I said:
'I am sorely afflicted,'
and when I said in my alarm:
'No man can be trusted.'

How can I repay the Lord
for his goodness to me?
The cup of salvation I will raise;
I will call on the Lord's name.

My vows to the Lord I will fulfil
before all his people.
O precious in the eyes of the Lord
is the death of his faithful.

Your servant, Lord, your servant am I;
you have loosened my bonds.
A thanksgiving sacrifice I make:
I will call on the Lord's name.

My vows to the Lord I will fulfil
before all his people,
in the courts of the house of the Lord,
in your midst, O Jerusalem.

Glory be...

Antiphon
You are my friends since you have remained in my love.

Reading

Ephesians 4:11-12

Some Christ has appointed to be apostles, others to be prophets, others to be evangelists, or pastors, or teachers. They

Radiating Christ

are to order the lives of the faithful, minister to their needs, build up the frame of Christ's body, until we all realise our common unity through faith in the Son of God, and fuller knowledge of him.

Short Responsory
℟ Tell of the glory of the Lord, announce it among the nations, alleluia.
℣ Speak of his wonderful deeds to all the peoples.
Glory be…

Benedictus/Magnificat Antiphon
Jesus saw a man called Matthew seated at the tax office and said to him, 'Follow me.' And he rose and followed him.

Benedictus (if said in the morning) or Magnificat (if said in the evening) - see inside front cover for these prayers

Intercessions
Since we are part of a building that has the apostles for its foundation, let us pray to the Father for his holy people.
℟ Lord, remember your Church.

Father, when your Son rose from the dead, you showed him first to the apostles; let us make him known, near and far.
℟ Lord, remember your Church.

You sent your Son into the world to proclaim the good news to the poor; grant that we may bring his gospel into the darkness of men's lives.
℟ Lord, remember your Church.

Our Father…

Concluding prayer
Lord,
you showed your great mercy to Matthew the tax-gatherer
by calling him to become your apostle.
Supported by his prayer and example may we always answer your call,
and live in close union with you.
Through Christ our Lord.
Amen.

Saint Matthew
Born at Capernaum. He was a tax gatherer when called by Jesus. He wrote his Gospel in the Hebrew language, and tradition has it that he preached the faith in the East.

Feast Day: 21 September

Radiating Christ

Tuesday - Mark
the 'winged lion': figure of courage and kingship

Introduction

O God, come to our aid. Lord, make haste to help us.

Glory be to the Father and to the Son and to the Holy Spirit, as it was in the beginning, is now, and ever shall be, world without end. Amen. (Alleluia)

omit Alleluias during Lent

Hymn

Let all on earth their voices raise,
re-echoing heaven's triumphant praise,
to him who gave the apostles grace
to run on earth their glorious race.

Thou art whose word they bore the light
of Gospel truth o'er heathen night,
to us that heavenly light impart,
to glad our eyes and cheer our heart.

Thou art whose will to them was given
to bind and loose in earth and heaven,
our chains unbind, our sins undo,
and in our hearts thy grace renew.

Thou in whose might they spake the word
which cured disease and health restored,
to us its healing power prolong,
support the weak, confirm the strong.

Antiphon

Through the gospel, God called us to faith in the truth so that we might share the glory of our Lord Jesus Christ, alleluia.

Psalmody

Psalm 125 (126)

When the Lord delivered Zion from bondage, it seemed like a dream.
Then was our mouth filled with laughter, on our lips there were songs.

The heathens themselves said: "What marvels the Lord worked for them!"
What marvels the Lord worked for us!
Indeed we were glad.

Deliver us, O Lord, from our bondage as streams in dry land.
Those who are sowing in tears will sing when they reap.

They go out, they go out, full of tears, carrying seed for the sowing:
they come back, they come back, full of song,
carrying their sheaves.

Glory be...

Antiphon

Through the gospel, God called us to faith in the truth so that we might share the glory of our Lord Jesus Christ, alleluia.

Reading
1 Corinthians 15:1-2a, 3-4

Brothers and sisters, I want to remind you of the gospel I preached to you, the gospel that you received and in which you are firmly established, because the gospel will save you. I taught you what I had been taught myself, namely that Christ died for our sins, in accordance with the scriptures; that he was buried, and that he was raised to life on the third day, in accordance with the scriptures.

Short Responsory
℟ They told of the glories of the Lord and of his might, alleluia.
℣ They spoke of the marvellous deeds he had done.
Glory be…

Benedictus/Magnificat Antiphon
Let us give thanks to Jesus Christ, who has sent teachers and evangelists to be ministers of faith to all peoples who believe in him, alleluia.

Benedictus (if said in the morning) or Magnificat (if said in the evening) - see inside front cover for these prayers

Intercessions
Our Saviour destroyed death and through the gospel revealed eternal life to us. With joyful praise let us make him know, and let us say.
℟ Strengthen your Church in faith and love.

Lord Jesus, in times past you have lighted the way for your people through wise and holy leaders; may Christians always enjoy this sign of your loving kindness.
℟ Strengthen your Church in faith and love.

You forgave the sins of your people when holy pastors prayed; continually cleanse your Church through their powerful intercession.
℟ Strengthen your Church in faith and love.

Our Father…

Concluding prayer
Almighty God,
you chose out the evangelist Saint Mark and ennobled him with grace to preach the gospel.
Let his teaching so improve our lives that we may walk faithfully in the footsteps of Christ.
Through Christ our Lord.
Amen.

Saint Mark
He was the cousin of Saint Barnabas. He accompanied Saint Paul the Apostle on his first missionary journey and later followed him to Rome. He was a disciple of Saint Peter and reproduced his teaching in his Gospel. He is said to have founded the Church of Alexandria.

Feast Day: 25 April

Wednesday - Luke
the 'winged bull': figure of sacrifice, service and strength

Introduction
O God, come to our aid. Lord, make haste to help us.

Glory be to the Father and to the Son and to the Holy Spirit, as it was in the beginning, is now, and ever shall be, world without end. Amen. (Alleluia)
omit Alleluias during Lent

Hymn
O fathers of our ancient faith,
with all the heav'ns we sing your fame
Whose sound went forth in all the earth
To tell of Christ, and bless his name.

You took the gospel to the poor,
The word of God alight in you,
Which in our day is told again:
That timeless word, for ever new.

You told of God who died for us
And out of death triumphant rose,
who gave the truth that made us free,
And changeless through the ages goes.

Praise Father, Son and Holy Ghost
Whose gift is faith that never dies:
A light in darkness now, until
The day-star in our hearts arise.
Stanbrook Abbey Hymnal

Antiphon
The holy evangelists sought out the wisdom of the ancients; in their gospels they confirmed the prophecies of old.

Psalmody
Canticle 21(Ephesians 1:3-10)
Blest be the God and Father
of our Lord Jesus Christ,
who has blessed us in Christ
with every spiritual blessing
in the heavenly places.

He chose us in him
before the foundation of the world,
that we should be holy
and blameless before him.

He destined us in love
to be his sons through Jesus Christ,
according to the purpose of his will,
to the praise of his glorious grace
which he freely bestowed on us in the
Beloved.

In him we have redemption through his blood,
the forgiveness of our trespasses,
according to the riches of his grace
which he lavished upon us.

He has made known to us
in all wisdom and insight
the mystery of his will,
according to his purpose
that he set forth in Christ.

His purpose he set forth in Christ
as a plan for the fullness of time,
to unite all things in him,
things in heaven and things on earth.

Antiphon
The holy evangelists sought out the wisdom of the ancients; in their gospels they confirmed the prophecies of old.

Radiating Christ

Reading *Romans 1:16-17*

I am not ashamed of the gospel. It is the saving power of God for everyone who has faith – the Jew first, but the Greek also – because here is revealed God's way of righting wrong, a way that starts from faith and ends in faith; as scripture says, 'he shall gain life who is justified through faith'.

Short responsory

℟ Their voice has gone out through all the earth.

℣ Their message reaches to the ends of the world.

Glory be…

Benedictus/Magnificat Antiphon

By giving us the gospel of Christ, Saint Luke proclaimed the rising of the Sun from on high.

Benedictus (if said in the morning) or Magnificat (if said in the evening) - see inside front cover for these prayers

Intercessions

Our Saviour destroyed death and through the gospel revealed eternal life to us. With joyful praise let us make him known, and let us say.

℟ Strengthen your Church in faith and love.

In the presence of their brothers, you anointed your holy ones and poured on them your Spirit; fill with your Holy Spirit all the leaders of your people.

℟ Strengthen your Church in faith and love.

Nothing could ever separate the holy pastors from your love; do not lose even one of those whom you redeemed by your passion.

℟ Strengthen your Church in faith and love.

Our Father…

Concluding prayer

Lord God,
you chose Saint Luke
to reveal the mystery of your love for the poor
  in his preaching and his writings.
Grant that those who already
  acknowledge your name
may continue to be one in mind and heart,
  and that all nations may see your salvation.
Through Christ our Lord.
Amen.

Saint Luke

Born of a pagan family and converted to the true faith, he was the companion of the apostle Paul and wrote his gospel in accordance with the apostle's preaching. He also wrote the account of the early days of the Church, up to the time of Paul's first stay in Rome, in the book called *The Acts of the Apostles.*

Feast Day: 18 October

Radiating Christ

Thursday - John
the 'eagle': soaring high, unflinchingly seeking God

Introduction
O God, come to our aid. Lord, make haste to help us.

Glory be to the Father and to the Son and to the Holy Spirit, as it was in the beginning, is now, and ever shall be, world without end. Amen. (Alleluia)
omit Alleluias during Lent

Hymn
Let all on earth their voices raise,
re-echoing heaven's triumphant praise,
to him who gave the apostles grace
to run on earth their glorious race.

Thou art whose word they bore the light
of Gospel truth o'er heathen night,
to us that heavenly light impart,
to glad our eyes and cheer our heart.

Thou art whose will to them was given
to bind and loose in earth and heaven,
our chains unbind, our sins undo,
and in our hearts thy grace renew.

Thou in whose might they spake the word
which cured disease and health restored,
to us its healing power prolong,
support the weak, confirm the strong.

Antiphon
This is John the virgin to whose trust
Christ, when he was dying on the Cross,
commended his mother, the Virgin Mary.

Psalmody
Psalm 62(63)

O God, you are my God, for you I long;
for you my soul is thirsting.
My body pines for you
like a dry, weary land without water.
So I gaze on you in the sanctuary
to see your strength and your glory.

For your love is better than life,
my lips will speak your praise.
So I will bless you all my life,
in your name I will lift up my hands.
My soul shall be filled as with a banquet,
my mouth shall praise you with joy.

On my bed I remember you.
On you I muse through the night
for your have been my help;
in the shadow of your wings I rejoice.
My soul clings to you;
your right hand holds me fast.

Antiphon
This is John the virgin to whose trust
Christ, when he was dying on the Cross,
commended his mother, the Virgin Mary.

Reading
2 Corinthians 5:19-20

God has entrusted to us the news that God and man are reconciled. so we are ambassadors for Christ; it is as though God were appealing through us, and the appeal that we make in Christ's name is: be reconciled to God.

Short Responsory

℟ You will make them rulers over all the land.

℣ Your name, Lord, will be remembered.

Glory be…

Benedictus/Magnificat Antiphon

The Word was made flesh and dwelt among us, and we saw his glory, alleluia.

Benedictus (if said in the morning) or Magnificat (if said in the evening) - see inside front cover for these prayers

Intercessions

Since we are part of that building which has the apostles for its foundation, let us pray to our Father for his holy people.

℟ Lord, remember your Church.

Father, you gave your Son to those in need; help us to bring the gospel to all.

℟ Lord, remember your Church.

Father, you sent to us your Word of life; may we labour to sow his word and reap a harvest of joy.

℟ Lord, remember your Church.

Father, your Son became our reconciliation; may we help to give peace to troubled hearts.

℟ Lord, remember your Church.

Our Father...

Concluding prayer

Almighty God,
who through your apostle John
unlocked for us the hidden treasures of
  your Word,
grant that we may grasp with fuller
  understanding
the message he so admirably proclaimed.
We make our prayer through Christ our
  Lord.
Amen.

Saint John

Son of Zebedee and brother of James, John worked as a fisherman on the shores of the Sea of Galilee. Initially a follower of John the Baptist, he was called by Jesus. After the Ascension, tradition holds that John worked in Jerusalem and at Ephesus. Lived into old age and died in AD99.

Feast Day: 27 December

Friday - Thus empowered, go and proclaim

Introduction

O God, come to our aid. Lord, make haste to help us.

Glory be to the Father and to the Son and to the Holy Spirit, as it was in the beginning, is now, and ever shall be, world without end. Amen. (Alleluia)

omit Alleluias during Lent

Hymn

Come, O Creator Spirit blest,
And in our souls take up Thy rest;
Come, with Thy grace and heavenly aid,
To fill the hearts which Thou hast made.

Great Comforter, to Thee we cry;
O highest gift of God most high,
O Fount of life, O Fire of love,
And sweet anointing from above!

The sacred sevenfold grace is Thine,
Dread finger of the hand divine;
The promise of the Father Thou,
Who dost the tongue with power endow.

Kindle our senses from above,
And make our hearts o'erflow with love;
With patience firm, and virtue high,
The weakness of our flesh supply.

Far from us drive the foe we dread,
And grant us Thy true peace instead;
So shall we not, with Thee for guide,
Turn from the path of life aside.

O may Thy grace on us bestow
The Father and the Son to know,
And evermore to hold confessed
Thyself of each the Spirit blest.

Antiphon

It is not you who will be speaking; the Spirit of your Father will be speaking in you, alleluia.

Psalmody

Psalm 109(110)

The Lord's revelation to my Master:
'Sit on my right:
your foes I will put beneath your feet.'

The Lord will yield from Zion
your sceptre of power:
rule in the midst of all your foes.

A prince from the day of your birth
on the holy mountains;
from the womb before the dawn I begot you.

The Lord has sworn an oath he will not change.
'You are a priest for ever,
a priest like Melchizedek of old.'

The Master standing at your right hand
will shatter kings in the day of his wrath.

He, the judge of the nations
will heap high the bodies;
heads shall be scattered far and wide.

He shall drink from the stream by the wayside
and therefore he shall lift up his head.

Antiphon

It is not you who will be speaking; the Spirit of your Father will be speaking in you, alleluia.

Reading   *2 Corinthians 1: 21-22*

If you and we belong to Christ, guaranteed as his and anointed, it is all God's doing; it is God also who has set his seal upon us, and as a pledge of what is to come has given the Spirit to dwell in our hearts.

Short Responsory

℟ They were all filled with the Holy Spirit, alleluia.

℣ They began to speak.

Glory be…

Benedictus/Magnificat Antiphon

Receive the Holy Spirit. Those whose sins you forgive will be forgiven them, alleluia.

Benedictus (if said in the morning) or Magnificat (if said in the evening) - see inside front cover for these prayers

Intercessions

Strengthened with measureless hope, we pray to Christ, who is calling his Church together in the Holy Spirit.

℟ Lord, renew the face of the earth.

Lord Jesus, raised on the cross, you poured out the water of rebirth for the life of the world. Quicken the life of all with the gift of the Spirit.

℟ Lord, renew the face of the earth.

You breathed your Spirit upon the apostles, and gave them the power of forgiveness: set us free from the prison of sin.

℟ Lord, renew the face of the earth.

You promised to send us the Spirit of truth, that we might become your heralds throughout the world. Through his presence in the Church may we bear fruitful witness to you.

℟ Lord, renew the face of the earth.

Our Father…

Concluding prayer

Lord God,
you sanctify your Church in every race
  and nation
by the mystery we celebrate at Pentecost.
Pour out the gifts of the Holy Spirit on all
  mankind,
and fulfil now in the hearts of your faithful
what you accomplished when the Gospel
  was first preached on earth.
Through Christ our Lord.
Amen.

The Calling of the Apostles Peter and Andrew
(1308-1311) by Duccio di Buoninsegna

Radiating Christ

Saturday - Making straight the paths

Introduction

O God, come to our aid. Lord, make haste to help us.

Glory be to the Father and to the Son and to the Holy Spirit, as it was in the beginning, is now, and ever shall be, world without end. Amen. (Alleluia)

omit Alleluias during Lent

Hymn

God called great prophets to foretell
The coming of his Son;
The greatest, called before his birth,
Was John, the chosen one.

John searched in solitude for Christ
And knew him when he came.
He showed the world the Lamb of God
And hailed him in our name.

That lonely voice cried out in truth,
Derided and denied.
As witness to the law of God
His mighty martyr died.

We praise you, Trinity in One,
The light of unknown ways,
The hope of all who search for you,
Whose love fills all our days.

Antiphon

He came as a witness to the truth.

Psalmody

Psalm 146(147)

Praise the Lord for he is good;
sing to our God for he is loving:
to him our praise is due.

The Lord builds up Jerusalem
and brings back Israel's exiles,
he heals the broken-hearted,
he binds up all their wounds.
He fixes the number of the stars;
he calls each one by its name.

Our Lord is great and almighty;
his wisdom can never be measured.
The Lord raises the lowly;
he humbles the wicked to the dust.
O sing to the Lord giving thanks;
sing psalms to our God with the harp.

His delight is not in horses
nor his pleasure in warriors' strength.
The Lord delights in those who revere him,
in those who wait for his love.

Antiphon

He came as a witness to the truth.

Reading
Isaiah 49:1, 5-6

Islands, listen to me, pay attention, remotest peoples. The Lord called me before I was born; from my mother's womb he pronounced my name. And now the Lord has spoken, he who formed me in the womb to be his servant: 'I will make you the light of the nations so that my salvation may reach to the ends of the earth.'

Short responsory

℟ Prepare a way for the Lord, make his paths straight.
℣ There is one coming after me who existed before me.

Glory be…

Benedictus/Magnificat Antiphon
Zachary opened his mouth and spoke
this prophecy: Blessed be the Lord, the
God of Israel.

Benedictus (if said in the morning)
or Magnificat (if said in the evening) -
see inside front cover for these prayers

Intercessions
Let us make our prayer to Christ who sent
John before him to prepare his way
℟ Lord, prepare us for your coming.

John showed in his life what he preached
by his words; give us the courage to
practise what we preach.
℟ Lord, prepare us for your coming.

John baptised you in the Jordan and the
Spirit of justice rested upon you; help us,
Lord, to work for a world of justice.
℟ Lord, prepare us for your coming.

Lord, you called men to preach your
word; send heralds to carry the gospel to
the world.
℟ Lord, prepare us for your coming.

Our Father…

Concluding prayer
Almighty God,
you sent John the Baptist to the people
   of Israel
to make them ready for Christ the Lord.
Give us the grace of joy in the Spirit,
and guide the hearts of all the faithful
in the way of salvation and peace.
Through Christ our Lord.
Amen.

Baptism of Christ (1622) by Guido Reni

Radiating Christ

Supplementary
resources

- Quotes for further reflection and prayers
- Exploring our Heritage
- Everyday Evangelising
- Summary of *Porta Fidei* (declaring the Year of Faith)
- My Family Tree (of Faith)
- Further reading

Quotes for further reflection

The Centrality of Jesus Christ
'It is Jesus that you seek when you dream of happiness; He is waiting for you when nothing else you find satisfies you; He is the beauty to which you are so attracted; it is He who provoked you with that thirst for fullness that will not let you settle for compromise; it is He who urges you to shed the masks of a false life; it is He who reads in your heart your most genuine choices, the choices that others try to stifle.

It is Jesus who stirs in you the desire to do something great with your lives, the will to follow an ideal, the refusal to allow yourselves to be ground down by mediocrity, the courage to commit yourselves humbly and patiently to improving yourselves and society, makng the world more human and more fraternal.'

Pope John Paul II, World Youth Day in Rome, 2000

The truth is that only in the mystery of the incarnate Word does the mystery of humankind take on light. For Adam, the first man, was a figure of Him Who was to come, namely Christ the Lord. Christ, the final Adam, by the revelation of the mystery of the Father and His love, fully reveals man to man himself and makes his supreme calling clear. It is not surprising, then, that in Him all the aforementioned truths find their root and attain their crown... For by His incarnation the Son of God has united Himself in some fashion with every person. He worked with human hands, He thought with a human mind, acted by human choice and loved with a human heart. Born of the Virgin Mary, He has truly been made one of us, like us in all things except sin.'

Pastoral Constitution on the Church in the Modern World - Gaudium et spes, 22

On Faith and Reason
'Faith and reason are like two wings on which the human spirit rises to the contemplation of truth; and God has placed in the human heart a desire to know the truth- in a word, to know himself- so that, by knowing and loving God, men and women may also come to the fullness of truth about themselves.'

Pope John Paul II - Fides et Ratio, 1998

The Essential Nature of the Church: Mission
'There is no doubt that the effort to proclaim the Gospel to the people of today, who are buoyed up by hope but at the same time often oppressed by fear and distress, is a service rendered to the Christian community and also to the whole of humanity.'

Paul VI - Evangelii Nuntiandi, 1

Radiating Christ

'At the same time, we Christians must never hesitate to proclaim our faith in the uniqueness of the salvation won for us by Christ.'

Pope Benedict XVI, Address at Lambeth Palace, 17 September 2010

'Evangelising is in fact the grace and vocation proper to the Church, her deepest identity. She exists in order to evangelise, that is to say, in order to preach and teach, to be the channel of the gift of grace, to reconcile sinners with God, and to perpetuate Christ's sacrifice in the Mass, which is the memorial of His death and glorious resurrection.'

Paul VI - Evangelii Nuntiandi, 14

'For by manifesting Christ, the Church reveals to men the real truth about their condition and their whole calling, since Christ is the source and model of that redeemed humanity, imbued with brotherly love, sincerity and a peaceful spirit, to which they all aspire. Christ and the Church, which bears witness to Him by preaching the Gospel, transcend every peculiarity of race or nation and therefore cannot be considered foreign anywhere or to anybody.'

Decree on the Mission Activity of the Church - Ad Gentes, 8

'…the Church cannot withdraw from the task of proclaiming Christ and his Gospel as saving truth, the source of our ultimate happiness as individuals and as the foundation of a just and humane society.'

Pope Benedict XVI, Reflection at Hyde Park, 18 September 2010

'All the members ought to be molded in the likeness of Him, until Christ be formed in them. For this reason we, who have been made to conform with Him, who have died with Him and risen with Him, are taken up into the mysteries of His life, until we will reign together with Him. On earth, still as pilgrims in a strange land, tracing in trial and in oppression the paths He trod, we are made one with His sufferings like the body is one with the Head, suffering with Him, that with Him we may be glorified.'

Dogmatic Constitution on the Church - Lumen Gentium , 7

On the Cross

'God's compassion for us is all the more wonderful because Christ died, not for the righteous or the holy but for the wicked and the sinful, and, though the divine nature could not be touched by the sting of death, he took to himself, through his birth as one of us, something he could offer on our behalf.'

Leo the Great (c.391 or 400-461)

Radiating Christ

Many indeed are the wondrous happenings of that time: God hanging from a cross, the sun made dark and again flaming out; for it was fitting that creation should mourn with its creator. The temple veil rent, blood and water flowing from his side: the one as from a man, the other as from what was above man; the earth shaken, the rocks shattered because of the rock; the dead risen to bear witness to the final and universal resurrection of the dead. The happenings at the sepulcher and after the sepulcher, who can fittingly recount them? Yet no one of them can be compared to the miracle of my salvation. A few drops of blood renew the whole world, and do for all men what the rennet does for the milk: joining us and binding us together.'

Gregory Nazianzen (c.329-389)

We adore you, Lord Jesus Christ,
in all the churches of the whole world
and we bless you, for by the means of your holy cross
you have redeemed the world.

St Francis of Assisi (1181-1226)

On Baptism and Keeping the Faith

Above all guard for me this great deposit of faith for which I live and fight, which I want to take with me as a companion, and which makes me bear all evils and despise all pleasures: I mean the profession of faith in the Father and the Son and the Holy Spirit. I entrust it to you today.'

Gregory Nazianzen (c.329-389)

Know ye not, that so many of us as were baptised into Jesus Christ were baptised into his death? Therefore we are buried with him by baptism into death: that like as Christ was raised up from the dead by the glory of the Father, even so we also should walk in newness of life. For if we have been planted together in the likeness of his death, we shall be also in the likeness of his resurrection.'

Romans 6:3-5 (KJV)

The earthly form of Christ is the form that died on the cross. The image of God is the image of Christ crucified. It is to this image that the life of the disciples must be conformed; in other words, they must be conformed to his death (Philippians 3.10, Romans 6.4) The Christian life is a life of crucifixion (Galatians 2.19) In baptism the form of Christ's death is impressed upon his own. They are dead to the flesh and to sin, they are dead to the world, and the world is dead to them (Galatians 6.14). Anybody living in the strength of Christ's baptism lives in the strength of Christ's death.'

Dietrich Bonhoeffer

Radiating Christ

'The Church does not dispense the sacrament of baptism in order to acquire for herself an increase in membership but in order to consecrate a human being to God and to communicate to that person the divine gift of birth from God.'

Hans Urs von Balthasar

'Jesus Christ was sent by the Father to proclaim the Gospel, calling all people to conversion and faith (cf. Mark 1:14-15). After his resurrection, he entrusted the continuation of his mission of evangelisation to the Apostles (cf. Matthew 28:19-20; Mark 16:15; Luke 24:4-7; Acts 1:3): "As the Father has sent me, so I send you" (John 20:21, cf. 17:18). By means of the Church, Christ wants to be present in every historical epoch, every place on earth and every sector of society, in order to reach every person, so that there may be one flock and one shepherd (cf. John 10:16): "Go out into the whole world and preach the Gospel to every creature. He who believes and is baptised will be saved, but he who does not believe will be condemned" (Mark 16:15-16).'

From Doctrinal Notes on Some Aspects of Evangelisation

Praying for the Lord's aid
My Lord and my God, take from me everything that distances me from you.
My Lord and my God, give me everything that brings me closer to you.
My Lord and my God, detach me from myself to give my all to you.

St Nicholas of Flüe (1417-1487)

O Lord Jesus Christ,
give us a measure of your Spirit
that we may be enabled to obey your teaching:
to pacify anger,
to take part in pity,
to moderate desire,
to increase love,
to put away sorrow,
to cast away vain glory,
not to be vindictive,
not to fear death;
ever entrusting our spirit to the immortal God
who with you and the Holy Spirit lives and reigns
world without end.

St Apollonius (170-245)

Lord Jesus Christ, Son of the living God, have mercy on me, a sinner.

The Jesus Prayer

Radiating Christ

Christ Pantokrator (c.1170) in the Basilica of Cefalù in Sicily – the icon for the Year of Faith. The text in Greek and Latin reads: 'I am the light of the world, who follows me will not wander in the darkness but will have the light of life' (John 8:12).

The Universal Prayer

Lord, I believe in you: increase my faith.
I trust in you: strengthen my trust.
I love you: let me love you more and more.
I am sorry for my sins: deepen my sorrow.

I worship you as my first beginning,
I long for you as my last end,
I praise you as my constant helper,
And call on you as my loving protector.

Guide me by your wisdom,
Correct me with your justice,
Comfort me with your mercy,
Protect me with your power.

I offer you, Lord, my thoughts:
to be fixed on you;
My words: to have you for their theme;
My actions: to reflect my love for you;
My sufferings: to be endured for your
greater glory.

I want to do what you ask of me:
In the way you ask,
For as long as you ask,
Because you ask it.

Lord, enlighten my understanding,
Strengthen my will,
Purify my heart,
and make me holy.

Help me to repent of my past sins
And to resist temptation in the future.
Help me to rise above my human
weaknesses
And to grow stronger as a Christian.

Let me love you, my Lord and my God,
And see myself as I really am:
A pilgrim in this world,
A Christian called to respect and love
All whose lives I touch,
Those under my authority,
My friends and my enemies.

Help me to conquer anger with gentleness
Greed by generosity,
Apathy by fervour.
Help me to forget myself
And reach out toward others.

Make me prudent in planning,
Courageous in taking risks.
Make me patient in suffering,
unassuming in prosperity.

Keep me, Lord, attentive at prayer,
Temperate in food and drink,
Diligent in my work,
Firm in my good intentions.

Let my conscience be clear,
My conduct without fault,
My speech blameless,
My life well-ordered.
Put me on guard against my human
weaknesses.

Let me cherish your love for me,
Keep your law,
And come at last to your salvation.

Teach me to realise that this world
is passing,
That my true future is the happiness
of heaven,
That life on earth is short,
And the life to come eternal.

Help me to prepare for death
With a proper fear of judgment,
But a greater trust in your goodness.
Lead me safely through death
To the endless joy of heaven.

Grant this through Christ our Lord.
Amen.

attributed to Pope Clement XI (1649-172

Radiating Christ

The Apostles' Creed

Also known as the Symbol of the Apostles, the Apostles' Creed is an early statement of Christian belief - possibly as early as c.180AD. The translation below is from the 2011 Roman Missal. The longer Nicene Creed can be found on page 24.

I believe in God,
the Father almighty,
Creator of heaven and earth,
and in Jesus Christ, his only Son, our Lord,
who was conceived by the Holy Spirit,
born of the Virgin Mary,
suffered under Pontius Pilate,
was crucified, died and was buried;
he descended into hell;
on the third day he rose again from the dead;
he ascended into heaven,
and is seated at the right hand of God the Father almighty;
from there he will come to judge the living and the dead.
I believe in the Holy Spirit,
the holy catholic Church,
the communion of saints,
the forgiveness of sins,
the resurrection of the body,
and life everlasting.
Amen.

Exploring our Heritage

Seti I and Ramese
build great cities
Nile Delta (1279-1

Wooden ships developed
in Crete (c.2000 BC)

Settlement in Melanesia
by immigrants from
Indonesia (c.2000 BC)

Stonehenge started in
Britain (c.2000 BC)

Domestication of the
horse (c.2000 BC)

Pharoah Tutankhamun
(1332-1322BC)

Start of the collapse of the
Bronze Age (c.1300BC)

Alphabetic writing
emerges (c.1800 BC)

Abraham leaves Ur
(c.1925BC)

King David (c.1040-
c.970BC)

Moses (c.1350-c.1230BC)

2000 BC

1000 BC

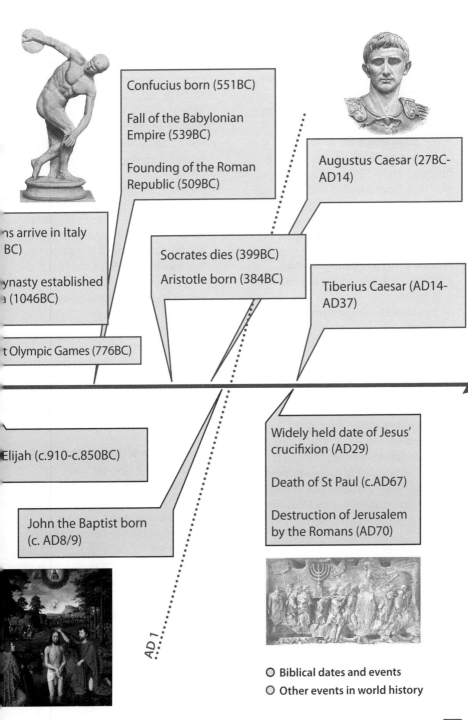

Confucius born (551BC)

Fall of the Babylonian Empire (539BC)

Founding of the Roman Republic (509BC)

Augustus Caesar (27BC-AD14)

...ns arrive in Italy ...BC)

...ynasty established ...a (1046BC)

Socrates dies (399BC)

Aristotle born (384BC)

Tiberius Caesar (AD14-AD37)

...t Olympic Games (776BC)

...Elijah (c.910-c.850BC)

Widely held date of Jesus' crucifixion (AD29)

Death of St Paul (c.AD67)

Destruction of Jerusalem by the Romans (AD70)

John the Baptist born (c. AD8/9)

AD 1

O Biblical dates and events
O Other events in world history

Radiating Christ

Everyday Evangelising

To evangelise is to share the Good News of Jesus, so the starting point for evangelisation is our relationship with Him. It's about proclaiming our faith in Him, by living it out in service and witness. We are called to share the story of Jesus in our lives, and then invite others to know Him too. These pages are taken from a leaflet designed to give Catholic individuals and communities practical ideas about how they can share their faith in Jesus in everyday life.

What is Everyday Evangelising?

- Everyday Evangelising is everyone's mission.
- By virtue of our Baptism, we are all called to share our faith.
- Everyday Evangelising is a way of life. It takes place at any time, in any place, under any circumstance.
- Everyday Evangelising reaches out to everyone. No one is excluded.
- Everyday Evangelising also addresses the social structures and communities that we find ourselves in: ' ...evangelising means bringing the Good News into all strata of humanity... transforming humanity from within and making it new' (EN, 18).

Being Prepared

- If we are introducing people to Jesus, we need to stay close to Him, and make sure that our own faith is being nurtured.
- Spend time in prayer daily.
- Read the Bible daily (for example the Gospel reading for the day).
- Receive the Sacraments.
- Fast periodically.

- Participate in a small Christian community or a parish prayer/Bible study group.
- Attend events, talks or courses to deepen your Christian faith.
- Read Catholic literature: magazines, books, or newspapers.

Everyday Evangelising in the Home

- Pray grace before and after meals.
- Proudly display symbols of our faith.
- Have a family calendar with the anniversary dates of reception of the Sacraments: Baptism, First Holy Communion, Marriage.
- Establish family rituals based on the Church year.
- Celebrate Church feast days, like the Feast of St Peter and St Paul , and your family feast days, like the days of the saints you're named after.
- Read together from the Bible.
- Discuss the morality of a TV show, or issues raised by news items.

Everyday Evangelising in the Parish

- Be gracious in the car park.
- Periodically sit in a different place in church and exchange names with those around you.
- Send a card to the newly baptised or confirmed.
- Pray for parish leaders and each other.
- Get involved in events and activities, if only on a small scale.
- Invite friends who aren't Catholic to parish events.
- Explain in advance to those who are not familiar with the Catholic Faith, what they will hear and see during the liturgies.

Taken from the Home mission Desk leaflet Everyday Evangelising for copies contact homemission@cbcew.org.uk

Everyday Evangelisation in the Workplace

- Transact all business dealings honestly
- Respect others' religious beliefs.
- Pray before making decisions.
- Offer to pray for a co-worker who has shared some personal concerns.
- Be ready to talk about the part Jesus plays in your life, and to be open about your Catholic faith (wear your Ash Wednesday ashes to work for example)
- Spend time with co-workers who share your Christian beliefs. Look for opportunities to pray together.

Everyday Evangelising by Social Justice

- Stay informed about the causes of poverty and war: log on to *www. justice-and-peace.org.uk* for links to organisations working on these issues.
- Bring this into prayer.
- Get involved: Is there a Justice and Peace, CAFOD or Pax Christi group in your parish you could join?
- Witness by the way you live: log on to *www.livesimply.org.uk* for steps you can take to live in a way that does justice to the poor and respects God's creation.

Everyday Evangelising for those Experiencing Stress

- Give ongoing support by offering a listening presence.
- Send a Mass card or a card of care and concern.
- Offer to pray with and for the person.
- Seek out agencies that can support them in their needs.

Everyday Evangelising in all Situations

- Respond with 'Thank God' when someone shares good news with you.
- Wear a cross or other symbol of your faith.
- Be ready for opportunities to share a story of how God works in your life.
- Ask people to pray for your intentions
- Invite to church those who have no faith community.
- Make the sign of the cross when dining out with friends and family.
- Share a smile and personal greeting.
- Share with neighbours about your parish.
- Without being a nuisance or a litter bug, leave religious materials in unexpected places.

Radiating Christ

Porta Fidei: a summary

provided by Fr Sergius Wroblewski, OFM

Porta Fidei is the apostolic letter by Pope Benedict XVI announcing the Year of Faith. Paragraphs as numbered in original document

1. **The 'door of faith'** (Acts 14:27) **is always open for us**, offering us the life of communion with God and offering entry into His Church when the Word of God is proclaimed and the heart allows itself to be transformed by grace. It begins with Baptism (cf. Romans 6:4); it is then that we can address God as Father. The end comes with the passage to eternal life.

2. **Ever since the start of my ministry** as the Successor of Peter, I have spoken of the need to rediscover the journey of faith. At the Mass inaugurating my pontificate, I said: 'The Church as a whole and all her Pastors, like Christ, must lead people out of the desert towards the place of life'. However, because so many think that faith is self-evident and its meaning and values have little appeal, a profound crisis of faith has affected many people.

3. **We cannot accept** that salt should become tasteless and the light be kept hidden (cf. Matthew 5:13-16). We must rediscover a taste for feeding ourselves on the Word of God and on the Bread of Life.

4. **In light of all this, I have decided to announce a Year of Faith.** It will begin on 11 October and it will end on the Solemnity of Christ our King on 24 November 2013. The starting date of 11 October 2012 also marks the 20th anniversary of the publication of the *Catechism of the Catholic Church*. This document was requested by the Extraordinary Synod of Bishops in 1985 to serve the catechists. Moreover, it was produced in collaboration with all the bishops of the Catholic Church. Moreover, I have convoked for 12 October 2012 the General Assembly of Bishops to consider the theme, 'THE NEW EVANGELIZATION FOR THE TRANSMISSION OF THE CHRISTIAN FAITH'. This will be a good opportunity to usher the whole Church into a time for the rediscovery of the Faith.

6. **The renewal of th** Church is also achieve through the witness offere by the lives of believer Christians are called t radiate the word of truth That requires conversio Hence, the Year of Faith a summons to an authenti and renewed conversion t the Lord, to conversion c life through the forgivenes of sins (cf. Acts 5:31). To th extent that he/she freel cooperates, one's thought and affections, mentalit and conduct are slowl purified and transformed.

7. **It is the love of Christ tha fills our hearts and impel us to evangelise.** Throug His love, Jesus attract to himself the people o every generation. Today there is need for stronge ecclesial commitmen to new evangelisatio in order to rediscove the joy of believin and the enthusiasm fo communicating the faith Faith grows when it i lived as an experience o love received and whe it is communicated as a experience of grace an joy. It makes us fruitfu and enables us to giv life-bearing witness. Onl through believing, ther does faith grow an become stronger.

. On this happy occasion, wish to invite my brother ishops from all over the world to join the Successor f Peter in recalling the recious gift of faith. We vill have the opportunity o profess our faith in ur cathedrals and in the hurches of the whole world; in our homes nd among our families. eligious communities as vell as parish communities re to find a way to make ublic profession of the redo.

0. At this point I would like o sketch a path intended o help us understand nore profoundly not only he content of the faith but lso the act of entrusting urselves fully to God. nowing the content to be elieved is not sufficient nless the heart which is he authentic sacred space vithin the person is opened y grace so as to see below he surface and understand he word of God. Moreover, Christian may never hink of belief as a private ct. Faith is choosing to tand with the Lord so as o live with him. Precisely ecause it is a free act, aith also demands social esponsibility for what one elieves. Finally, profession f faith is both personal and communitarian. As we read in the Catechism of the Catholic Church: "'I believe" is the faith of the Church professed personally by each believer, principally during baptism. "We believe" is the faith of the Church confessed by the bishops assembled in council or more generally by the liturgical assembly of believers.' That said, we must not forget that very many people are sincerely searching for the definitive truth of their lives and of the world.

11. To arrive at a systematic knowledge of the content of the faith, all can find in the *Catechism of the Catholic Church* an indispensable tool. Blessed John Paul II called it a 'valid and legitimate instrument for ecclesial communion and a sure norm for teaching the faith.'

14. **The Year of Faith will also be a good time to intensify the witness of charity**. Faith without charity bears no fruit. Without faith charity would be a sentiment constantly at the mercy of doubt. Did not James write: 'But someone will say, "You have faith and I have works." Show me your faith apart from your works, and I by my works will show you my faith' (James 2:14-18). Therefore faith and charity require each other.

15. **May this Year of Faith make our relationship with Christ increasingly firm**, because only He guarantees an authentic and lasting love. We believe with firm certitude that the Lord Jesus has conquered evil and death. With confidence we entrust ourselves to him: he, present in our midst overcomes the power of the evil one (cf. Luke 11:20); and the Church, the visible community of his mercy, abides in him as a sign of definitive reconciliation with the Father. Let us entrust this time of grace to the Mother of God, proclaimed 'blessed because she believed' (Luke 1:45).

Given in Rome at Saint Peter's on 11 October in the year 2011, the seventh of the pontificate of Benedict XVI.

We are all encouraged to read *Porta Fidei* as part of the Year of Faith. The full letter can be found on the Vatican's Year of Faith website:
www.annusfidei.va

My Family Tree (of Faith)

**Those who helped me
in my faith journey**

My name

**Those who I am called to
help in their faith journey**

You may wish to continue on a separate sheet!

Further reading

Church Documents

Ad Gentes (Second Vatican Council decree Decree on the Missionary Activity of the Church) - http://goo.gl/6aKpX

Evangelii Nuntiandi (Paul VI's apostolic letter on the proclamation of the gospel) - http://goo.gl/WyNdc

Redemptoris Missio (John Paul II's encyclical on the permanent validity of the Church's missionary mandate) - http://goo.gl/itEQn

Disciples Called to Witness: The New Evangelization - http://goo.gl/lSfGX

Year of Faith

The Bishops' Conference of England & Wales has developed a website with focuses on parish renewal and the Synod of bishops due to take place in Rome on the New Evangelisation at the start of the Year of Faith - www.yearoffaith.org.uk

The Pontifical Council for Promoting the New Evangelisation has created a wonderful website with video catechesis, resources and information on the council itself - www.annusfidei.va/content/novaevangelizatio/en.html

The US Bishops' Conference has aggregated a lot of content on a new webpage: www.usccb.org/beliefs-and-teachings/how-we-teach/new-evangelization/year-of-faith/ including a Catholic basics section *Rediscovering The Faith*

You can also listen to a talk given by the current and first President of the Pontifical Council for the Promotion of the New Evangelisation, Archbishop Rino Fisichella, on the Church's Gospel mission 50 years after the Second Vatican Council by visiting this link - http://goo.gl/9gxTM

After the season has finished, you may also be interested in:

Why Catholic? RENEW International's new programme, using the small group model, offers a rich scriptural and catechetical approach that provides a solid foundation for every Catholic to express their faith and be able to reach out to others. Its 48 sessions are based on the four pillars of the Catechism: beliefs, sacraments, morality, and prayer. For more see - www.whycatholic.org/

For Notes